*Countries Around the World*

# United States of America

Michael Hurley

**Ⓡ** www.raintreepublishers.co.uk
Visit our website to find out
more information about
Raintree books.

**To order:**
☎ Phone 0845 6044371
▤ Fax +44 (0) 1865 312263
▣ Email myorders@raintreepublishers.co.uk

Customers from outside the UK please telephone +44 1865 312262

Raintree is an imprint of Capstone Global Library Limited,
a company incorporated in England and Wales having its
registered office at 7 Pilgrim Street, London, EC4V 6LB –
Registered company number: 6695582

Text © Capstone Global Library Limited 2012
First published in hardback in 2012
Paperback edition first published in 2013
The moral rights of the proprietor have been asserted.

Edited by Catherine Veitch and Charlotte Guillain
Designed by Steve Mead
Original illustrations © Capstone Global Library Ltd 2012
Illustrated by Oxford Designers & Illustrators
Picture research by Hannah Taylor
Originated by Capstone Global Library Ltd
Printed in China by CTPS

ISBN 978 1 406 23538 8 (hardback)
16 15 14 13 12
10 9 8 7 6 5 4 3 2 1

ISBN 978 1 406 23545 6 (paperback)
17 16 15 14 13 12
10 9 8 7 6 5 4 3 2 1

**British Library Cataloguing in Publication Data**
Hurley, Michael
United States of America. -- (Countries around the world)
973.9'32-dc22
A full catalogue record for this book is available from the
British Llibrary.

**Acknowledgements**
We would like to thank the following for permission to
reproduce photographs: Corbis pp. 12 (Wally McNamee),
13 (Bob Adelman), 23 (Tyrone Turner/National Geographic
Society), 26 (Robin Nelson/ZUMA Press), 29 (Tom Fox/Dallas
Morning News), 31 (Hulton-Deutsch Collection), 32 (Bett-
mann), 35 (Irwin Thompson/Dallas Morning News); Getty
Images pp. 7 (Bridgeman Art Library), 22 (AFP/Saul Loeb), 34
(Joe Robbins); Istockphoto pp. 15 (© Richard Gunion), 16 (©
Tomasz Szymanski), 27 (© jabejon); The Kobal Collection p. 33
(UNIVERSAL/DREAMWORKS); Library of Congress pp. 9, 10,
11; Shutterstock pp. 5 (© Songquan Deng), 6 (© stocksnapp), 8
(© Susan Law Cain), 19 (© egd), 20 (© Ferenc Cegledi), 21 (©
Andrew S.), 25 (© Christopher Halloran), 39 (© S.Borisov).

Cover photograph of the Statue of Liberty reproduced with
permission of Corbis (Cameron Davidson).

Every effort has been made to contact copyright holders of
any material reproduced in this book. Any omissions will
be rectified in subsequent printings if notice is given to
the publisher.

The publishers would like to thank Dr Elizabeth Clapp and
Marta Segal Block for their assistance in the preparation of this
book. The author would also like to thank Catherine Clarke for
her assistance with this book.

# Contents

Some words in the book are in bold, **like this**. You can find out what they mean by looking in the glossary.

# Introducing the United States of America

What comes to mind when you think about the United States of America? Do you see the United States flag with its stars and stripes? Do you think of big cities with dramatic skyscrapers? Perhaps you are familiar with US culture from watching films and television programmes?

## North America

The United States is.an enormous and varied country. Its stunning scenery includes dramatic coastlines, mountain ranges, forests, deserts, rivers, and lakes. The United States is part of the **continent** of North America, which also includes Canada and Mexico. After Canada, the United States is the second largest country on the continent. It has an area of more than 9,826,675 square kilometres (3,794,100 square miles). The population of the United States is approximately 307 million, making it the third most populated country in the world. The country has a huge diversity of culture, with people from all round the world settling there.

## Superpower

The United States is often referred to as a superpower. This relates to the strength of its government and its influence over the rest of the world. In terms of size, population, and **economy**, the United States has been a very powerful country for over a century. The United States is often at the forefront of international campaigns, whether in response to a natural disaster such as an earthquake, or to the outbreak of war between two countries. This influence on a global scale creates both positive and negative feelings towards the country.

Many of the cities in the United States have amazing skylines full of tall buildings.

# History: exploration, colonization, and conflict

Humans have lived in the land that is now the United States for more than 12,000 years. Over time these people settled all over what is now North America. These people, who later became known as American Indians, or Native Americans, lived here for thousands of years before other settlers arrived on the **continent**.

## Daily life

American Indians made tools and hunted for food. Coastal people lived on a diet of mainly fish, while inland tribes hunted animals such as **bison** (buffalo) for meat. Different tribes developed their own religions and cultures.

## Discovering a "new world"

From the 1400s, explorers like Christopher Columbus set off from Europe. They explored new lands in the Caribbean and the coasts of Central and South America. In 1497 John Cabot, an Italian navigator sailing on a British ship, became the first European to visit the northeast coast of North America since the Vikings in AD 1000.

## Colonization

The first permanent British settlement in North America was Jamestown, which was founded in 1607 in present-day Virginia. Between 1620 and 1630 more **colonists** arrived on the north-eastern coast. The British people who **migrated** here were known as Puritans. They wanted to come to this new land because they thought that they would be free to practise their religion in their own way.

The early colonists faced many hardships and dangers. Food was often scarce and disease was common. They also came into conflict with American Indian people. The American Indians helped and supported the colonists until their lands and way of life became threatened. Eventually, the colonists managed to establish farms and plantations.

This is an artist's impression of an early British settlement on the east coast of North America.

On 4 July 1776, during the Revolutionary War, the colonists declared their independence.

## The American Revolution

The new settlers built up thriving settlements, and began to resent the restrictions imposed on their freedom by the British. On 19 April 1775, the Revolutionary War began between the Americans and the British. In 1783, the Americans finally defeated the British.

## Territorial expansion

In 1803 the United States bought land from the French in the Louisiana Purchase. For about $15 million, the United States acquired land that went from New Orleans in the south to Montana in the north. This encouraged more American citizens to move westward.

War broke out between the United States and Mexico in 1846 over land ownership and boundaries. US forces invaded Mexico and eventually gained lands that included present-day New Mexico and California. The United States now controlled land from the east coast to the west coast.

## Civil War (1861–1865)

From the 1500s, many Africans were taken from their homes and forced to work in the growing European settlements in North America. By the 1800s, slavery was a part of life in the United States, and it became a major factor in the most devastating war in US history.

The Civil War ripped the nation in half. The southern Confederate states fought to protect slavery and break away from the northern states. The northern Union states wanted to preserve the union and end slavery. This terrible war divided the country, and families and friends fought on opposite sides. More than 620,000 soldiers were killed.

## HARRIET TUBMAN

### (ABOUT 1820-1913)

Harriet Tubman was an escaped slave. She helped many other slaves to escape to freedom in the North and Canada. During the Civil War, she served as a nurse and spy for the Union army.

## Boom time

There were huge developments in industry after the Civil War. An increase in machine-operated manufacturing was driven by new inventions and railway networks. The industrial growth caused a boom in the **economy** that continued into the 20th century.

## World War I

The United States stayed out of World War I at first, but President Wilson and the American people were moved to join the war against Germany in 1917. Around two million soldiers were sent across the Atlantic to help the **Allies** to victory in 1918.

## The 1920s and the Great Depression

The 1920s is often known as the "Roaring Twenties", because of its booming economy and fast-paced life. But by the end of the 1920s, the spectacular economic growth had become unstable, and in 1929 the **stock market** crashed.

During the Great Depression in the 1930s, people were forced to queue for hours to get food.

During the Great Depression, which followed this crash, banks failed, millions of workers lost their jobs, and thousands of farmers were forced to abandon their farms. In 1933, around 13 million Americans were out of work.

## World War II

The United States initially stayed out of World War II. However, in 1941 a devastating Japanese attack on a US naval base at Pearl Harbor brought the country into the war. At the time of the attack, Japan's ally, Germany, had taken over much of Europe. So the United States joined the Allies, which included the United Kingdom and the **Soviet Union**, to defeat their enemies. The war ended in 1945 when the United States dropped **atomic** bombs on two Japanese cities, Hiroshima and Nagasaki.

The surprise attack on Pearl Harbor by the Japanese cost over 2,000 American lives. It led directly to the United States' involvement in World War II (1939–1945).

## The Cold War and Vietnam

Following World War II, a Cold War developed between the **capitalist** and **communist** nations of the world. This tension was mainly between the United States and the Soviet Union. The Cold War led to conflict in other countries, where the United States was eager to prevent the rise of communism. One of the major conflicts was the Vietnam War (1954-75). Thousands were killed in this war and many Americans protested against it.

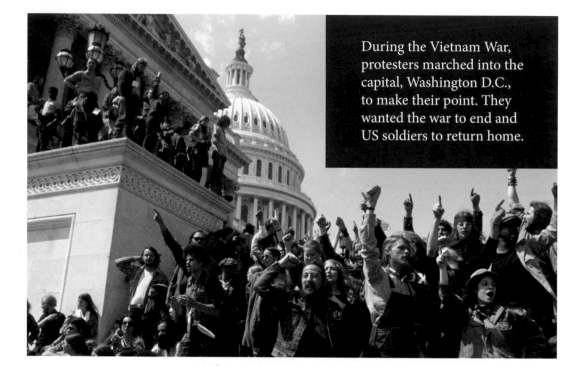

During the Vietnam War, protesters marched into the capital, Washington D.C., to make their point. They wanted the war to end and US soldiers to return home.

## JOHN F. KENNEDY (1917–1963)

John F. Kennedy was the youngest man ever to be elected as president of the United States, and was also the youngest to die in office. He was assassinated in 1963, and the nation mourned the passing of a popular young leader.

# Civil rights

After the end of the Civil War and the **abolition** of slavery, **segregation** laws remained in the United States, including the "Jim Crow laws" in the southern states. These laws prevented white and black people from using the same public places, such as public toilets and drinking fountains.

In 1955, in Alabama, an African American woman named Rosa Parks refused to give up her seat on a public bus for a white person. She was arrested and fined, creating headlines across the country. This started a **civil rights** movement to end segregation. For many years the fight for civil rights was led by Dr Martin Luther King, Jr. He encouraged people to protest peacefully rather than turn to violence. Tragically he was **assassinated** in 1968. Gradually, attitudes changed, and in 2008 the people of the United States elected their first non-white president, Barack Obama.

The 1960s were a time of turmoil in the United States. There were many protest marches by African Americans trying to get equal rights.

# Regions and resources: mountains, manufacturing, and movies

The United States is the third largest country in the world by area. It has a land border with Canada to the north, and Mexico to the south. Two of the states, Alaska and Hawaii, are not physically linked to the rest of the United States. Alaska is in the far northwest of North America, bordering Canada, and Hawaii is an island group in the Pacific Ocean.

## Climate

Due to the size of the country, the climate in the United States varies greatly from region to region. From the hot and dry deserts of Arizona, to the freezing sub-arctic landscape of Alaska, the United States has almost every type of climate there is on Earth! The United States is used to extreme weather, including hurricanes and tornadoes.

This map shows the physical features, such as mountains and rivers, of the United States.

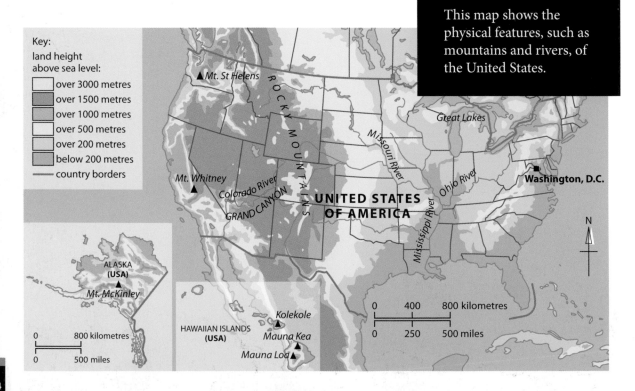

Key:
land height above sea level:
- over 3000 metres
- over 1500 metres
- over 1000 metres
- over 500 metres
- over 200 metres
- below 200 metres
- —— country borders

Mt. St Helens
ROCKY MOUNTAINS
Great Lakes
Missouri River
Mt. Whitney
Colorado River
GRAND CANYON
Ohio River
Washington, D.C.
UNITED STATES OF AMERICA
Mississippi River
N

ALASKA (USA)
Mt. McKinley
0     800 kilometres
0     500 miles

HAWAIIAN ISLANDS (USA)
Kolekole
Mauna Kea
Mauna Loa

0     400     800 kilometres
0     250     500 miles

# Key landforms

The landscape of the United States includes mountains and tropical areas, as well as huge plains and large deserts. It has one of the longest coastlines in the world.

The Grand Canyon, in Arizona, is one of the most spectacular landforms in the world. It was formed over millions of years by the Colorado River. The canyon extends 446 kilometres (277 miles), and is approximately 1.6 kilometres (1 mile) deep. At 6,194 metres (20,322 feet), the country's highest mountain is Mount McKinley, in Alaska.

Mount McKinley was named after US President William McKinley. The Athabaskan Indians of Alaska, however, called the mountain Denali, which means "The Great One" or "The High One".

## United States

Fifty states make up the United States of America. Alaska is the largest state, with an area of 1,530,699 square kilometres (591,006 square miles). Alaska is more than twice the size of the next largest state, Texas. The smallest state is Rhode Island, with an area of 3,139 square kilometres (1,212 square miles). Each state has its own identity, including its own capital city and flag.

## Major cities

The capital city of the United States is Washington, D.C. It is home to many important government buildings, including the White House, the residence of the president of the United States. The two largest cities in the United States are New York City, on the east coast, and Los Angeles in California, on the west coast. Both cities have large, **multicultural** populations.

The United States' third largest city is Chicago. Chicago is in the state of Illinois, on the edge of Lake Michigan. Chicago is a beautiful city, with lakefront beaches, large parks, and the world famous Art Institute of Chicago.

Chicago is known as the "Windy City". This is because of the strong winds that blow off Lake Michigan.

## How to say...

As people from the United States come from all over the world, many languages are spoken. The most commonly spoken languages are Spanish, Chinese, **Tagalog**, Vietnamese, and French. Here are some basic greetings in Spanish:

| | | |
|---|---|---|
| hello | *hola* | (oh-lah) |
| goodbye | *adiós* | (ah-dee-os) |
| my name is… | *mi llamo…* | (may yamo) |
| thank you | *gracias* | (grah-see-ahs) |
| good night | *buenos noches* | (bway-nos no-chays) |

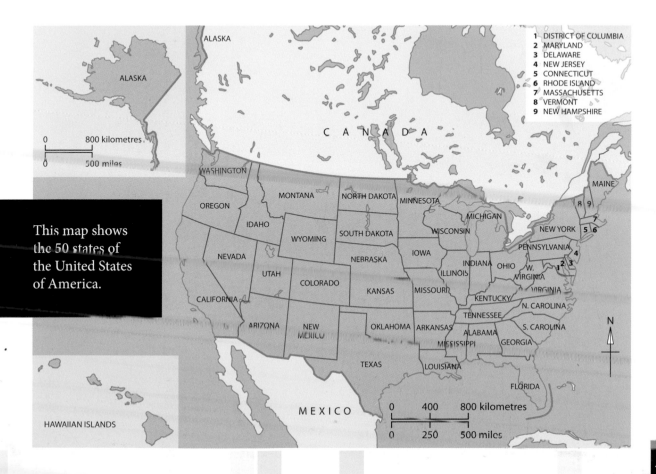

This map shows the 50 states of the United States of America.

1  DISTRICT OF COLUMBIA
2  MARYLAND
3  DELAWARE
4  NEW JERSEY
5  CONNECTICUT
6  RHODE ISLAND
7  MASSACHUSETTS
8  VERMONT
9  NEW HAMPSHIRE

ALASKA

ALASKA

0    800 kilometres
0    500 miles

CANADA

WASHINGTON
OREGON
MONTANA
NORTH DAKOTA
MINNESOTA
IDAHO
WYOMING
SOUTH DAKOTA
WISCONSIN
MICHIGAN
MAINE
NEW YORK
NEVADA
NEBRASKA
IOWA
PENNSYLVANIA
UTAH
COLORADO
KANSAS
MISSOURI
ILLINOIS
INDIANA
OHIO
W. VIRGINIA
VIRGINIA
KENTUCKY
CALIFORNIA
ARIZONA
NEW MEXICO
OKLAHOMA
ARKANSAS
TENNESSEE
N. CAROLINA
S. CAROLINA
ALABAMA
MISSISSIPPI
GEORGIA
TEXAS
LOUISIANA
FLORIDA

N

MEXICO

0    400    800 kilometres
0    250    500 miles

HAWAIIAN ISLANDS

17

# Economy

The United States' **economy** is one of the strongest in the world. There are many different industries in different parts of the country.

# Manufacturing

Traditionally, large parts of the **Midwest** region of the United States were industrial areas, producing steel, cars, and machinery. The city of Detroit in Michigan, for example, produces more cars each year than any other part of the country, and is known as "Motor City". The city's location on the Detroit River played a large part in its rapid growth, as it was cheap and easy to transport **raw materials** to Detroit.

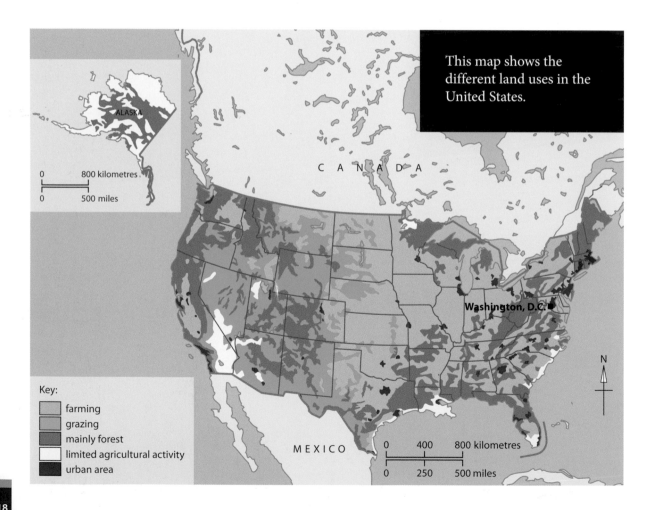

This map shows the different land uses in the United States.

Key:
- farming
- grazing
- mainly forest
- limited agricultural activity
- urban area

## Agriculture

Alongside manufacturing, agriculture still remains a huge industry for the United States. Kansas is one of the largest producers of wheat in the country and is often called the "Breadbasket of America". The fertile soil and rich mineral deposits make Kansas an ideal farming area, and farmland covers 90 per cent of the state, including around 63,000 farms.

## Sunshine industry

The west coast of the United States is perhaps most famous for its film industry. Hollywood, in California, became a centre of the film industry because it has a mild, dry climate, and it lies in an area with a huge variety of natural scenery that can be used for filming. The film industry contributes millions of dollars to the US economy each year. California is also home to "Silicon Valley". This is the leading computer-manufacturing region of the country, and includes the headquarters of hundreds of computer and electronics companies, such as Apple and Hewlett-Packard.

Hollywood, California, is one of the most famous and fascinating places on Earth.

# Wildlife: diversity and disasters

Due to the country's size and the different types of land and climate across the United States, there is a rich variety of plant and animal life.

In Alaska, for example, there is a great diversity of arctic wildlife. The region is home to 180 bird species, around 45 types of land and marine mammals (including grizzly and polar bears), and more than 35 types of fish. Many of these animals are not found anywhere else in the United States. Unfortunately, the natural habitats in this area are under threat from climate change and the activities of oil companies.

In the far south of the United States, in Florida, the Everglades are home to very different wildlife. Plant life ranges from saw grass to mangrove swamps. Animals in the Everglades include alligators, heron, pelicans, and snakes. There is also the rare Florida panther to look out for!

Alligators live in swamps in Florida and Louisiana, in the southern United States. These alligators are often hunted for their meat and their skin.

## National parks

There are national parks all over the United States. These parks are areas specifically set up to protect the natural environment. There are 393 parks in 49 states, covering a total area of 339,936 square kilometres (131,250 square miles). In 2009 there were almost three million visitors to the national parks.

Yellowstone National Park stretches across three states: Wyoming, Montana, and Idaho. Visitors can see animals such as wolves, **bison**, elk, and grizzly bears in their natural environment. Another big draw for visitors are the amazing **geysers** that spray hot water from underground up into the air.

People travel from all over the world to visit Yellowstone National Park. They want to catch a glimpse of the largest geyser "Old Faithful" in action.

## Environmental disasters

Two of the most damaging environmental disasters in US history have involved oil spills. In 1989 the *Exxon Valdez* oil tanker struck a reef in Prince William Sound, Alaska, spilling nearly 42 million litres (11 million gallons) of oil into the sea. This destroyed wildlife and polluted beaches and fishing waters. Scientists are still working to restore the ecological balance in this area.

On 20 April 2010, the Deepwater Horizon oil rig in the Gulf of Mexico exploded, killing 11 workers. It then sank, causing 5,000 barrels of oil per day to leak into the ocean. Wildlife, including brown pelicans, ducks, turtles, and whales, were affected as they got caught up in the slick, and coastal industries were severely affected.

A volunteer at the Fort Jackson Oiled Wildlife Rehabilitation Center in Buras, Louisiana, cleans an oil-covered pelican. It was found off the Louisiana coast.

## Pollution and waste

**Fossil fuels** are fuels such as coal and oil that are burned for fuel. When they are burned, they give off harmful substances like carbon dioxide, which are called greenhouse gases. Scientists believe that greenhouse gases lead to global warming, a worldwide rise in temperatures. The United States releases more carbon dioxide than any other country in the world. As a result, there is increasing pressure for the country to find ways to reduce this problem.

Like many other **developed countries**, the United States creates a huge amount of waste. A US citizen creates two to three times the amount of waste as a person living in a **developing country**. In 2005 the United States created 223 million tonnes of rubbish! However, recycling has increased, and from 1990 to 2005 the amount of waste going to landfills decreased by 8 million tonnes. Environmentalists want to see more people recycling, composting, and reusing their rubbish.

It is very important that families recycle as much waste as possible.

# Infrastructure: leaders, health, and schools

The system of government in the United States divides power between the national government and individual state governments. This is called a federal system. Each state has many powers that would be the responsibility of the national government in many countries. For example, states are responsible for creating most laws, including setting their own state taxes.

## BARACK OBAMA (BORN 1961)

Barack Obama is the first non-white president of the United States. He was born to a Kenyan father and white American mother in Hawaii. Obama worked as a state senator in Illinois and as a US senator from Illinois, before becoming the Democratic Party's nominee for the 2008 presidential election.

## National government

The two main political parties in the United States are the Republican Party and the Democratic Party. Every four years, a person is chosen to represent these two parties and they compete for the presidency. Third party candidates often also enter the race. Once elected, a president can be in power for no more than two terms, for a maximum of eight years.

The United States **Congress** is made up the House of Representatives and the **Senate**. The Senate has 100 members, two from each state, and the House of Representatives has 435. The number of members from each state in the House of Representatives is based on the size of each state's population.

## Healthcare

In the United States people pay for their own healthcare. This is done by buying insurance, which helps pay for medication and treatment. Many people have insurance through their jobs, but others do not have insurance and cannot afford medical care. The US government is currently trying to change this.

United States president Barack Obama is shown here, addressing the nation.

SEAL OF THE PRESIDENT OF THE UNITED STATES

# School life

Each state has control over its own education system, and decides what pupils will study at school. At the age of five, many children start kindergarten. This prepares children for school. From the age of six children begin more formal education, studying subjects such as maths, science, and social studies. They then go on to either a middle school or a junior high school.

Children study the required subjects of English, maths, science, and health at high school. Additionally, they can choose some classes from either a "college preparatory" or a **vocational** curriculum.

Many school children start their day in class by reciting the "Pledge of Allegiance", which is a solemn promise to be loyal to their country, while saluting the nation's flag.

These pupils are reciting the Pledge of Allegiance at the start of a school day.

## Daily life

The school day usually starts at 8.00 a.m. and ends at about 3.00 p.m. Many schools operate a school bus service to take children to and from school. The yellow school bus is a familiar sight, and is something that is recognized around the world as a symbol of US school life.

## College and university

High school is the end of **compulsory** education in the United States, but some students continue their education at college or university. The United States has some famous universities, including Harvard and Yale. Many students who cannot afford to go to university or who are not academically ready, start at a junior college and later transfer to a larger university.

# Culture: food, sport, and entertainment

For many generations, people have moved to the United States in search of opportunity. This has created a **multicultural** population with a rich mixture of customs and cultures.

## Food

Many large American cities have areas called "Chinatown" or "Little Italy", where restaurants serve food from those countries. There is a culture of eating out, with hundreds of restaurants in every city. Some are fast food restaurants. People also often cook at home. People have family meals at home to celebrate special occasions, such as Thanksgiving, or have cook-outs (barbecues) during the summer.

### Chocolate brownies

Ask an adult to help you make these delicious treats.

**Ingredients**

- 50 grams softened margarine
- 50 grams sugar
- 50 grams unsweetened cocoa powder
- 1 egg
- 100 grams plain flour
- 25 grams chopped walnuts

**What to do**

1. Preheat oven to 180°Celsius (350°Farenheit).
2. Lightly grease an 8 centimetre (3.5 inch) by 20 centimetre (7.5 inch) baking tray.
3. Cream the margarine and sugar together in a large bowl.
4. Mix in the cocoa powder, then add the egg and beat the mixture for about 1–2 minutes, until smooth and combined.
5. Sift the flour and add to the mixture, then stir in the nuts.
6. Evenly spread the mixture into the tin and bake for 18–20 minutes.
7. Cool and then cut into squares.

## Sport

Many major US cities have professional sports teams that play baseball, American football, basketball, and ice hockey. Fans enthusiastically follow these teams. Each sport has a season and these seasons overlap so there is always sport being played. Each sport has an end-of-season game, or series of games, to decide who is the overall winner for the year. In baseball this is called the World Series, while in American football it is the Super Bowl.

### MICHAEL JORDAN (BORN 1963)

Michael Jordan is one of the best known sportsmen in the United States. He was the most influential and talented player for the Chicago Bulls basketball team. His team won six National Basketball Association (NBA) titles.

The United States has many great athletes who compete on a world stage, in competitions such as the Olympics.

## Music

The United States has a very rich musical history. The earliest popular music was traditional folk music, which originated in Europe and other parts of the world. Musical styles that first appeared in the United States include gospel, jazz, country, blues, and rock'n'roll.

In the 1950s and 1960s, rock'n'roll was popular. Elvis Presley became famous around the world. Modern music has many different cultural influences. Rap music and r'n'b include songs that tell stories about **urban** life. Dance music and pop music are still very popular with people of all ages and backgrounds.

## Theatre

The most famous theatre district in the United States is Broadway in New York. Many plays and long-running musicals are put on here, attracting New Yorkers and out-of-town visitors alike. This theatre district has its own annual awards ceremony, the Tony Awards, which honours achievement in areas such as acting, directing, designing, musical arrangements, and choreography (creating dance routines).

## Visual art

Andy Warhol and Jackson Pollock are two famous US artists. Both were controversial figures during their careers, but are now considered two of the greatest 20th-century artists. Warhol's prints present everyday objects, such as tins of soup, in a new and visually stimulating way. Pollock's style used aggressive strokes and paint dripped directly onto canvas.

This is Ella Fitzgerald recording one of her songs. She made her first recording, called "Love and Kisses", in 1935.

# ELLA FITZGERALD (1917–1996)

Ella Fitzgerald, known as "the first lady of song", was one of the greatest jazz singers of all time. She was popular with people of different races, ages, and backgrounds. In a career that lasted more than 50 years she sold over 40 million albums and won many awards.

## Film

Films are a huge part of the American way of life. Many films are made in Hollywood. The first films were black and white silent films that were usually comedies. As technology moved on, sound and colour were introduced. From musicals to westerns, Hollywood produced some of the best-known and best-loved films of all time.

## WALT DISNEY (1901–1966)

Cartoons and animated films have always been popular, and none more so than those created by Walt Disney. He created characters such as Mickey Mouse and Donald Duck. His full-length films, including *Fantasia*, *The Jungle Book*, and *Mary Poppins*, helped him to win an amazing 32 **Academy Awards**!

One of the most successful films of all time was the 1939 epic, *Gone with the Wind*, which was set against the backdrop of the Civil War. This film was based on a novel by US author Margaret Mitchell.

# Literature

One of the best-known 19th-century authors is Mark Twain, who wrote *The Adventures of Huckleberry Finn*. Millions of children and adults have enjoyed these adventures set along the Mississippi River.

Louisa May Alcott's novel *Little Women* tells the story of a group of sisters growing up in New England in the mid-1800s. It has been made into several films.

From *The Grinch* to *The Cat in the Hat*, children's author Dr Seuss created some of the best-loved characters in literature. His clever rhyming text and funny illustrations have charmed many children over the years, and in 1984 the Pulitzer Prize Board awarded him a Special Citation "for his contribution over nearly half a century to the education and enjoyment of America's children and their parents".

Dr. Seuss' creation *The Cat in the Hat* was turned into a film in 2003.

# The United States today

The United States is an ever-changing country, and its major cities continue to grow in size and population. The influx of people from other countries through immigration means that the cities' populations are very diverse.

The United States is a very strong country from a political point of view. It is a member of the **G8** and the **United Nations**. It works closely with other **developed countries** to find solutions to worldwide problems such as famine and terrorism. The United States also has an important trade agreement with Canada and Mexico. This ensures fairness for the three countries in terms of the **import** and **export** of their goods.

Many Americans are proud of their country. The national anthem, the "Star Spangled Banner", is sung before all major sporting events.

## Resilience

The people of the United States often show strength in the face of challenges. When disaster strikes, they come together to help each other.

The events of 11 September 2001, when four aeroplanes were hijacked by **terrorists**, were the first time since the Japanese attack on Pearl Harbor that the United States had been attacked on home soil. The destruction caused by planes flying into the World Trade Center in New York and the **Pentagon** sent shockwaves through the country, and the world. The ability of the American people, particularly New Yorkers, to withstand such a tragic event and continue with their lives has shown their great determination and courage.

After Hurricane Katrina devastated the city of New Orleans in 2005, people from all over the world helped to raise money to assist those affected.

Many thousands of people in New Orleans were made homeless because of the devastating impact of the flooding after Hurricane Katrina.

# Fact file

| | |
|---|---|
| **Official name:** | United States of America |
| **Official language:** | English (Hawaiian is the official language of the state of Hawaii) |
| **Capital city:** | Washington, D.C. |
| **Bordering countries:** | Canada; Mexico |
| **Population:** | 307,226,000 |
| **Largest cities and population:** | New York (8,391,881); Los Angeles (3,831,868); Chicago (2,851,268); Houston (2,257,926) |
| **Urban population:** | 82% |
| **Birth rate:** | 13.83 per 1,000 people |
| **Life expectancy:** | 78.1 years (total); 75.7 years (men); 80.7 years (women) |
| **Ethnic groups:** | White 79.96% (including 16.3% Hispanic); Black 12.85%; Asian 4.43%; American Indian and Alaska Native 0.97%; Hawaiian 0.18%; Other 1.61% |
| **Religion:** | Protestant 51.3%; Roman Catholic 23.9%; None 12.1%; Mormon 1.7%; Jewish 1.7%; Other 9.3% |
| **Internet users:** | 231,000,000 |
| **Military service:** | voluntary |
| **Type of government:** | **constitution**-based federal **republic** |
| **National animal:** | American buffalo |
| **National tree:** | oak |
| **Climate:** | temperate (mild); tropical in Hawaii and Florida; arctic in Alaska |
| **Total area:** | 9,826,675 square kilometres (3,794,100 square miles) |
| **Land area:** | 9,161,966 square kilometres (3,537,455 square miles) |
| **Water area:** | 664,709 square kilometres (256,646 square miles) |
| **Mountains:** | McKinley; Whitney; St. Helens |
| **Major rivers:** | Missouri; Mississippi; Colorado; Ohio |
| **Highest elevation:** | Mount McKinley 6,194 metres (20,322 feet) |
| **Lowest elevation:** | Death Valley 86 metres (282 feet) below sea level |
| **Currency:** | US dollar ($) |

| | |
|---:|:---|
| **Resources:** | coal; copper; lead; gold; iron; mercury; oil; natural gas; timber |
| **Major industries:** | petroleum; steel; vehicles; aerospace; telecommunications; chemicals; electronics; food processing |
| **Imports:** | clothing; furniture; toys; oil; vehicles |
| **Exports:** | transistors; aircraft; vehicle parts; fruit; soya beans; corn; computers; medicines |
| **Units of measurements:** | imperial |

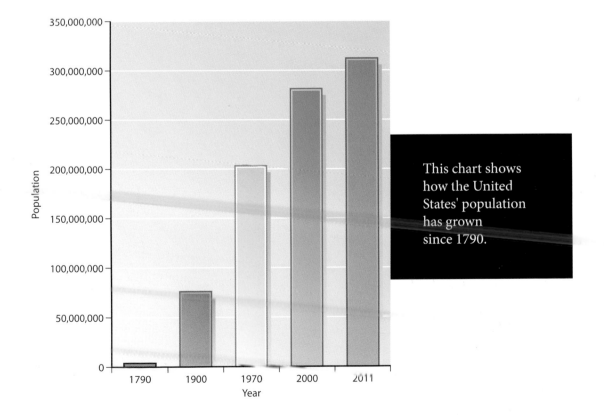

This chart shows how the United States' population has grown since 1790.

## Famous Americans

Mohammed Ali (boxer); Neil Armstrong (astronaut); Hillary Clinton (politician); Tom Cruise (actor); Amelia Earhart (aviation pioneer); Thomas Edison (inventor); Bill Gates (businessman); LeBron James (basketball player); Billie Jean King (tennis player); Martin Luther King, Jr (**civil rights** activist); Beyonce Knowles (singer/songwriter); Abraham Lincoln (politician); Barack Obama (politician); Rosa Parks (civil rights activist); Elvis Presley (singer/songwriter); Franklin D. Roosevelt (politician); Pete Sampras (tennis player); Elizabeth Cady Stanton (women's rights activist); Mark Twain (author); George Washington (politician); Oprah Winfrey (television personality).

## National anthem

The United States national anthem is called the "Star Spangled Banner". It was written during the war of 1812, based on words written by Francis Scott Key. The United States **Congress** made the song the official national anthem in 1931.

*Oh, say, can you see, by the dawn's early light,*

*What so proudly we hail'd at the twilight's last gleaming?*

*Whose broad stripes and bright stars, thro' the perilous fight,*

*O'er the ramparts we watch'd, were so gallantly streaming?*

*And the rocket's red glare, the bombs bursting in air*

*Gave proof thro' the night that our flag was still there.*

*Oh, say, does that Star-Spangled Banner yet wave*

*O'er the land of the free and the home of the brave?*

# National holidays

1 January – New Year's Day
3rd Monday in January – Martin Luther King Day
3rd Monday in February – Presidents' Day
30 May – Memorial Day
4 July – Independence Day
1st Monday in September – Labor Day
2nd Monday in October – Columbus Day
11 November – Veterans' Day
4th Thursday in November – Thanksgiving
25 December – Christmas Day

Fireworks light up the sky over the capital during the annual 4th of July (Independence Day) celebrations.

# Timeline

BC is short for "before Christ". BC is added after a date and means that the date occurred before the birth of Jesus Christ, for example, 450 BC.

AD is short for Anno Domini, which is Latin for "in the year of our Lord". AD is added before a date and means that the date occurred after the birth of Jesus Christ, for example, AD 720.

| | |
|---|---|
| about 20000–35000 BC | The first residents of North America arrive over the Bering Strait |
| 1492 | Christopher Columbus discovers the "new world" |
| 1565 | First permanent European settlement in North America, founded by the Spanish |
| 1607 | Jamestown, Virginia, founded by British settlers |
| 1773 | During the "Boston tea party", **colonists** dump British tea into Boston harbour in protest against British taxes |
| 1775 | George Washington is appointed to lead the fight against British rule. The Revolutionary War begins. |
| 1776, 4 July | Thomas Jefferson's American Declaration of Independence is approved by **Congress**; colonies declare independence |
| 1783 | The Americans defeat the British; the Revolutionary War ends |
| 1787 | The Founding Fathers draw up a new **constitution** for the United States of America; the Constitution comes into effect in 1788 |
| 1789 | George Washington is elected first US President |
| 1803 | The Louisiana Purchase doubles the size of the United States |
| 1808 | The slave trade is **abolished** in the United States |
| 1846–1848 | The United States acquires vast areas of Mexican territory, including present-day California and New Mexico, after the Mexican-American War |
| 1860–1861 | Eleven pro-slavery southern states **secede** from the Union and form the Confederate States of America, triggering the Civil War |
| 1863 | President Abraham Lincoln issues the Emancipation Proclamation, declaring slaves in the Confederate states free |

| | |
|---|---|
| 1865 | The Civil War ends; the Confederates are defeated; slavery is abolished. Lincoln is **assassinated** |
| 1876 | Sioux Indians defeat US troops at Little Big Horn |
| 1890 | US troops defeat Sioux Indians at Wounded Knee |
| 1917 | The United States joins the **Allies** to fight in World War I. |
| 1930s | About 13 million people become unemployed after the Wall Street **stock market** crash triggers what becomes known as the Great Depression |
| 1941 | Japanese warplanes attack the US fleet at Pearl Harbor in Hawaii; United States declares war on Japan and enters World War II |
| 1945 | The United States drops two **atomic** bombs on Hiroshima and Nagasaki; Japan surrenders. World War II ends. |
| 1950–1953 | US forces play a leading role against North Korean and Chinese troops in the Korean War |
| 1954 | As a result of the "Brown versus Board of Education of Topeka" case, racial **segregation** in schools is declared unconstitutional. A movement to gain **civil rights** for African Americans begins. |
| 1963 | President John F. Kennedy is assassinated |
| 1968 | The civil rights leader Dr Martin Luther King Jr. is assassinated |
| 1969 | The United States lands people on the moon for the first time |
| 1975 | After almost 20 years of fighting, the Vietnam War ends |
| 1991 | The United States and allied forces attack Iraq in response to the Iraqi invasion of Kuwait |
| 2001 | **Terrorists** attack the United States and destroy the World Trade Center, over 3,000 people die. The United States invades Afghanistan in response. |
| 2008 | Barack Obama is elected the 44th US President |

# Glossary

**abolition** removal or ending

**Academy Awards** prestigious yearly award ceremony for the film industry

**Allies** during World Wars I and II, the group of countries that included the United Kingdom, France, and eventually the United States; the Allies fought against Germany

**assassinated** killed suddenly or secretively, usually for political reasons

**atomic** relating to the energy of atoms when they are split

**bison** large mammal closely related to cattle

**capitalist** economic system where production and distribution are privately owned, and prices are determined by competition in a free market

**civil rights** the right to be treated fairly, regardless of your sex, colour, or religion

**colonist** person who arrives to settle in a new country

**communist** economic system where all means of production and distribution, and all natural resources, belong to the state

**compulsory** required by rules or laws

**Congress** the branch of US government that is elected to make laws

**constitution** set of basic laws by which a country is governed

**continent** one of the Earth's seven major areas of land

**developed country** country or part of the world with an economy that is more advanced than some other parts of the world

**developing country** a country or part of the world with an economy that is not as advanced as some other parts of the world

**economy** to do with money and the industry and jobs in a country

**export** sell goods to another country

**fossil fuel** substance such as coal or oil that is burned for fuel

**G8** group of industrialized countries, including the United States, Canada, the United Kingdom, and Germany

**geyser** hot spring that shoots hot water and steam into the air from under the surface

**import** buy goods from another country

**indigenous** originating in, and characteristic of a particular region or country

**Midwest** region of the United States, including the states of Illinois, Minnesota, and Indiana

**migrate** move from one area to another, to find work or settle

**multicultural** representing many different cultures

**NBA** the National Basketball Association

**Pentagon** building that houses the main offices for the armed services of the United States

**raw material** natural substance that other things are made from

**republic** country where there is an elected government and no king or queen

**secede** withdraw from a group or political union

**segregation** separating people, usually in racial groups

**Senate** one half of the US Congress, made up of two senators from each state; the other half of Congress is the House of Representatives

**Soviet Union** group of countries, including Russia, that made up the Union of Soviet Socialist Republics (USSR)

**stock market** market where shares in businesses are traded

**Tagalog** language spoken by many people from the Philippines and other areas. Sometimes referred to as "Filipino".

**terrorist** person who uses violence to achieve a political aim

**United Nations** global organization formed in 1945 to promote peace and security

**urban** to do with a town or city

**vocational** relating to an educational course that provides skills needed for a particular profession

# Find out more

## Books

*Children's Encyclopedia of American History*, David C. King
   (Dorling Kindersley, 2003)
*Little Women*, Louisa M. Alcott (Penguin Classics, 2007)
*Martin Luther King Jr.: A Dream of Hope*, Alice Fleming (Sterling, 2008)
*National Geographic Countries of the World: United States*, Elden Croy
   (National Geographic Society, 2010)
*North American Indian*, David Hamilton Murdoch (Dorling Kindersley, 2005)
*The Adventures of Huckleberry Finn*, Mark Twain (Penguin Classics, 2007)

## Websites

**kids.nationalgeographic.com/kids/places/find/united-states-of-america/**
Find games, videos, and articles all about the United States here.

**kids.yahoo.com**
Type "United States" into this search engine and find lots of photos, videos, and articles, as well as links to other great sites about the United States.

**www.usa4kids.com**
This website provides interesting information about the United States. You can find out about all of the individual states, where they are located in the United States and what each state flag looks like. There is also a detailed timeline to help you find out about the history of the United States.

## Places to visit

### The Grand Canyon, Arizona
See the amazing natural beauty of the Grand Canyon from above by taking a trip on a helicopter. Afterwards you can ride the rapids on the Colorado River at the bottom of the Canyon.

### Mount Rushmore, South Dakota

The faces of four US Presidents - George Washington, Thomas Jefferson, Theodore Roosevelt, and Abraham Lincoln - can be seen carved into the rock face of Mount Rushmore.

### California's golden beaches

You can have a go at body boarding or surfing on one of the many golden beaches on the California coast.

### Kennedy Space Center, Cape Canaveral, Florida

If you are lucky, you might get to see a rocket setting off on a space mission from the world famous Kennedy Space Center.

## Further research

What did you find interesting in this book? Is there something that you would like to know more about? Here are some topics that you might like to research further:

- Find out about the native peoples and their history, customs, and religions.
- Find out more about slavery in the United States. How did it start and why? How long did it last? And when was slavery stopped?
- Choose one of the 50 states and find out more about the people who live there, their traditions, different cuisines, and read about the interesting places to visit.

You could find out more about the United States of America by visiting your local library, looking at the websites listed here, or actually visiting the country yourself.

# Topic tools

You can use these topic tools for your school projects. Trace the map onto a sheet of paper, using the thick black outline to guide you.

The United States flag is called the "Stars and Stripes", and it is easy to see why. Each star represents a state, so there are 50 in all. The 13 stripes represent the 13 original colonies. The flag is sometimes referred to as "Old Glory". Copy the flag design and then colour in your picture. Make sure that you use the right colours!

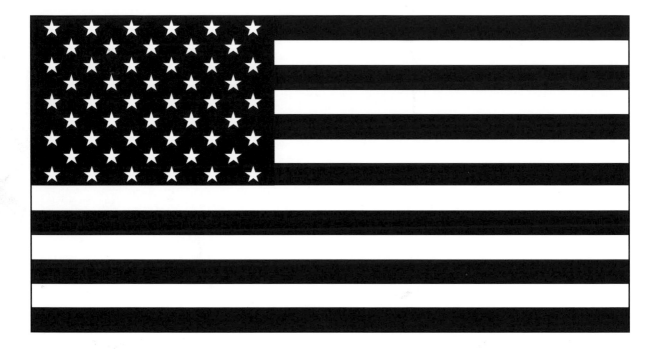

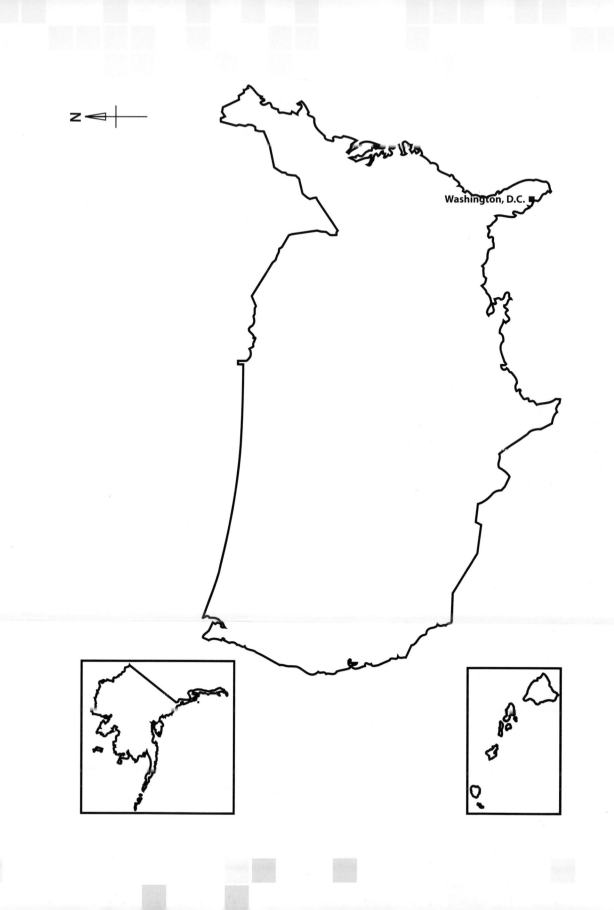

Washington, D.C. ■

# Index